# Tiny Shifts in Habit for Big Results

*The 4 Laws*

Mike Bhangu

BBP Copyright 2025

Copyright © 2025 by Mike Bhangu.

This book is licensed and is being offered for your personal enjoyment only. It is prohibited for this book to be re-sold, shared and/or to be given away to other people. If you would like to provide and/or share this book with someone else, please purchase an additional copy. If you did not personally purchase this book for your own personal enjoyment and are reading it, please respect the hard work of this author and purchase a copy for yourself.

All rights reserved. No part of this book may be used or reproduced or transmitted in any manner whatsoever without written permission from the author, except for the inclusion of brief quotations in reviews, articles, and recommendations. Thank you for honoring this.

_____

Published by BB Productions
British Columbia, Canada
thinkingmanmike@gmail.com

# Tiny Shifts in Habit for Big Results

## *The 4 Laws*

"Tiny Shifts in Habit for Big Results", focuses on the power of incremental improvements, habit formation, and sustainable growth.

## *Table of Contents*

Introduction: The Power of Tiny Shifts

Chapter 1: How Habits Shape Your Identity

Chapter 2: The Habit Loop: Cue, Routine, Reward

Chapter 3: The Myth of Willpower

Chapter 4: Law 1 – Make It Obvious

Chapter 5: Law 2 – Make It Attractive

Chapter 6: Law 3 – Make It Easy

Chapter 7: Law 4 – Make It Satisfying

Chapter 8: Breaking Bad Habits

Chapter 9: Dealing with Setbacks

Chapter 10: From Tiny Shifts to Big Results

Chapter 11: Building Systems, Not Goals

Conclusion: The Ripple Effect of Tiny Shifts

# Introduction: The Power of Tiny Shifts

### The Story of the 1% Rule

Imagine two people standing at the base of a mountain. One decides to climb just 1% higher each day, while the other waits for the perfect moment to make a giant leap. At first, the difference between them seems negligible. But over time, the person making tiny, consistent shifts begins to rise steadily, while the other remains stuck at the bottom, waiting for a breakthrough that never comes.

This is the essence of Tiny Shifts: the idea that small, incremental changes, when applied consistently, can lead to extraordinary results. Whether it's improving your health, building a successful career, or strengthening relationships, the key lies not in dramatic overhauls but in the daily habits that shape your life.

### Why Big Goals Often Fail

We've all been there: setting ambitious New Year's resolutions, only to abandon them by February. Why does this happen? The problem isn't a lack of desire or effort—it's the approach. Big goals often feel overwhelming, and when progress isn't immediate, it's easy to lose motivation.

Research shows that 80% of New Year's resolutions fail by mid-February, and the reason is simple: we focus on the destination rather than the journey. We set lofty goals without creating a system of habits to support them. But what if the secret to success wasn't about setting bigger goals but about making smaller, smarter changes?

## The Science of Small Changes

The power of tiny shifts isn't just a motivational idea—it's rooted in science. Consider the concept of compound interest: just as a small amount of money grows exponentially over time, small improvements compound into massive results. For example:

- If you improve by just 1% each day, you'll be 37 times better by the end of the year.
- Conversely, if you decline by 1% each day, you'll nearly disappear.

This principle applies to every area of life. Whether it's learning a new skill, building a business, or improving your health, small, consistent actions create a ripple effect that leads to lasting change.

## The Problem with Overnight Success

In a world obsessed with instant gratification, we're often sold the myth of overnight success. Social media showcases people's highlight reels, making it seem like success happens overnight. But the truth is, real change is a slow, gradual process.

Think of a bamboo tree: for the first few years, it shows no visible growth. But beneath the surface, its roots are growing deep and strong. Then, suddenly, it shoots up to incredible heights. Similarly, the tiny shifts you make today may not seem significant, but they're laying the foundation for future success.

**The 4 Laws of Tiny Shifts**

This book is built on a simple, actionable framework called The 4 Laws of Tiny Shifts:

1. Make It Obvious: Design your environment to highlight the habits you want to build.
2. Make It Attractive: Pair habits with rewards to make them more appealing.
3. Make It Easy: Reduce friction and start small to build momentum.
4. Make It Satisfying: Celebrate small wins to reinforce positive behavior.

These laws are based on the latest research in psychology, neuroscience, and behavioral science. They provide a roadmap for creating habits that stick and breaking ones that don't.

**What You'll Learn in This Book**

This book is designed to be a practical guide for anyone looking to make lasting changes in their life. Here's what you can expect:

- The Foundation of Habits: Understand how habits work and why they're so powerful.
- The 4 Laws of Tiny Shifts: Learn how to create and sustain habits using a proven framework.
- Overcoming Obstacles: Discover strategies for breaking bad habits and staying on track.

- Scaling Your Habits: See how small changes can lead to big results over time.

Each chapter includes real-life examples, actionable strategies, and exercises to help you apply the concepts to your own life.

**The Ripple Effect of Tiny Shifts**

The beauty of tiny shifts is that they don't just change one area of your life—they create a ripple effect. When you start exercising regularly, you might notice improvements in your energy, mood, and productivity. When you develop a habit of reading, you might find yourself thinking more creatively and making better decisions.

Small changes don't just add up—they multiply. And over time, they can transform not just your habits but your identity. As the philosopher Aristotle once said, "We are what we repeatedly do. Excellence, then, is not an act but a habit."

**A Call to Action**

The journey of a thousand miles begins with a single step. You don't need to have it all figured out to start making changes. In fact, the best way to make progress is to start small and build momentum.

As you read this book, I encourage you to take action. Don't just consume the information—apply it. Experiment with the strategies, reflect on what works for you, and keep iterating. Remember, the goal isn't perfection—it's progress.

**Final Thought**

Tiny shifts may seem insignificant at first, but their power lies in their consistency. By focusing on small, manageable changes, you can create a life of purpose, growth, and fulfillment. The journey won't always be easy, but it will be worth it.

So, are you ready to start making tiny shifts? Let's begin.

# Chapter 1: How Habits Shape Your Identity

### The Story of Two Runners
Imagine two people who decide to start running.
- Runner A sets a goal: "I want to run a marathon." They focus on the outcome, pushing themselves to train hard every day. But when progress feels slow, they get discouraged and eventually quit.
- Runner B takes a different approach. Instead of focusing on the marathon, they focus on becoming a runner. They start small, running just 10 minutes a day, and gradually build their habit. Over time, they not only complete a marathon but also adopt a new identity: "I am a runner."

This story illustrates a fundamental truth: habits are not just actions—they are a reflection of who you are. To create lasting change, you must start by changing your identity.

### The Connection Between Habits and Identity
Your habits are more than just routines; they are votes for the type of person you want to become. Every time you choose to read a book instead of scrolling through social media, or to eat a healthy meal instead of junk food, you are casting a vote for your desired identity.

- Outcome-Based Habits: Focus on what you want to achieve (e.g., losing weight, saving money).

- Identity-Based Habits: Focus on who you want to become (e.g., a healthy person, a financially responsible individual).

The problem with outcome-based habits is that they rely on external motivation, which often fades. Identity-based habits, on the other hand, are driven by internal beliefs. When you see yourself as the type of person who values health, productivity, or growth, your habits naturally align with that identity.

**The Two-Step Process for Changing Your Identity**

Changing your identity might sound daunting, but it's a simple two-step process:

1. Decide Who You Want to Be: What kind of person do you want to become? What values do you want to embody?
2. Prove It to Yourself with Small Wins: Take small actions that reinforce your desired identity. Each action is a vote for your new self.

For example, if you want to become a writer, start by writing one paragraph a day. Over time, these small wins will add up, and you'll begin to see yourself as a writer.

**The Role of Belief in Habit Formation**

Belief is the foundation of identity change. You can't adopt a new habit if you don't believe it's possible. This is why small wins are so powerful—they provide evidence that you're capable of change.

- The Power of Evidence: Every time you complete a small habit, you gather evidence that supports your new identity. For example, if you want to become a morning person, waking up early even once is proof that you can do it.
- The Danger of Negative Beliefs: If you believe you're "bad at math" or "not a creative person," you'll struggle to adopt habits that contradict those beliefs. To change your habits, you must first change your beliefs.

**Practical Exercise: Define Your Desired Identity**

To start building identity-based habits, take a moment to reflect on who you want to become. Use the following prompts to guide your thinking:

1. What are your core values? What kind of person do you want to be?
2. What habits align with those values? For example, if you value health, what habits would a healthy person have?
3. What small actions can you take today? What's one tiny shift you can make to start living out your desired identity?

Write down your answers and keep them somewhere visible. This will serve as a reminder of the person you're working to become.

**Case Study: The Power of Identity Change**

Consider the story of Sarah, a woman who struggled with procrastination. For years, she told herself, "I'm just a lazy person." But when she decided to change her identity, everything shifted.

- Step 1: Decide Who You Want to Be: Sarah decided she wanted to be a productive, disciplined person.
- Step 2: Prove It with Small Wins: She started by completing one small task each day, like making her bed or writing a to-do list. Over time, these small wins reinforced her new identity.

Within a few months, Sarah had transformed her habits—not because she set bigger goals, but because she changed how she saw herself.

**The Compound Effect of Identity-Based Habits**

When you focus on identity, your habits become more than just actions—they become a reflection of who you are. And as you accumulate small wins, your confidence grows, making it easier to tackle bigger challenges.

- Example: If you see yourself as a reader, you'll naturally gravitate toward books instead of TV. If you see yourself as a healthy person, you'll choose nutritious foods without thinking twice.

Over time, these small shifts compound into massive results. But the real magic lies in the fact that you're not just changing your habits—you're changing yourself.

**A Call to Action**

The journey of habit change begins with a single question: Who do you want to be? Take a moment to reflect on your desired identity and write down one small habit that aligns with it. Remember, you don't need to be perfect—you just need to start.

As you move through this book, keep your identity in mind. Every habit you build is a vote for the person you want to become. And with each tiny shift, you're one step closer to making that identity a reality.

**Final Thought**

Habits are the building blocks of identity. By focusing on who you want to be, rather than what you want to achieve, you create a foundation for lasting change. So, who do you want to become? And what tiny shift will you make today to start becoming that person?

# Chapter 2: The Habit Loop: Cue, Routine, Reward

### The Story of the Morning Coffee

Imagine this: Every morning, you wake up, stumble into the kitchen, and brew a cup of coffee. The smell of coffee fills the air, and as you take that first sip, you feel a sense of calm and readiness for the day ahead.

This simple ritual is an example of a habit loop—a three-part process that governs how habits form and persist. Understanding this loop is the key to unlocking the power of habits, both good and bad.

### What Is the Habit Loop?

The habit loop, a concept popularized by Charles Duhigg in *The Power of Habit*, consists of three components:

1. Cue: The trigger that initiates the habit.
2. Routine: The behavior or action you perform.
3. Reward: The benefit or satisfaction you gain from the behavior.

These three elements work together to create automatic behaviors. Over time, the loop becomes so ingrained that the behavior feels effortless—and sometimes even unconscious.

### The Science Behind the Habit Loop

The habit loop is rooted in neuroscience. When you perform a habit, your brain releases dopamine, a neurotransmitter associated with pleasure and reward. This dopamine release reinforces the behavior, making you more likely to repeat it in the future.

- Cue: The cue activates the brain's habit center, the basal ganglia, which stores automatic behaviors.
- Routine: The routine is the action itself, which becomes more automatic with repetition.
- Reward: The reward satisfies a craving, creating a positive feedback loop that strengthens the habit.

Understanding this process allows you to hack your habits—either by creating new ones or breaking old ones.

**Breaking Down the Habit Loop**

*1. The Cue: What Triggers Your Habits?*
Cues are the signals that prompt your brain to initiate a habit. They can be external (like a time of day or a location) or internal (like an emotion or thought). Common types of cues include:
- Time: Habits tied to specific times of day (e.g., brushing your teeth before bed).
- Location: Habits triggered by specific places (e.g., snacking while watching TV).
- Emotional State: Habits tied to emotions (e.g., stress eating).
- Other People: Habits influenced by social interactions (e.g., smoking with friends).
- Immediately Preceding Action: Habits linked to a previous behavior (e.g., checking your phone after waking up).

Practical Exercise: Identify the cues for one of your habits. Ask yourself:
- When does this habit usually occur?
- Where does it happen?
- What emotions or thoughts precede it?

*2. The Routine: The Behavior Itself*

The routine is the action you take in response to the cue. This is the most visible part of the habit loop, but it's only one piece of the puzzle.

- Good Habits: Productive routines, like exercising or meditating.
- Bad Habits: Negative routines, like procrastinating or overeating.

The key to changing habits is not just to focus on the routine but to understand the cue and reward that drive it.

*3. The Reward: Why You Repeat the Behavior*

Rewards are the reason habits stick. They satisfy a craving, whether it's physical (e.g., the taste of food), emotional (e.g., stress relief), or psychological (e.g., a sense of accomplishment).

- Immediate vs. Delayed Rewards: Habits are more likely to stick when the reward is immediate. For example, the immediate pleasure of eating junk food often outweighs the long-term benefits of eating healthy.
- Intrinsic vs. Extrinsic Rewards: Intrinsic rewards (e.g., feeling proud) are more sustainable than extrinsic rewards (e.g., earning money).

Practical Exercise: Identify the reward for one of your habits. Ask yourself:
- What craving does this habit satisfy?
- How does it make me feel?

**How to Hack the Habit Loop**

Once you understand the habit loop, you can use it to your advantage. Here's how:
1. Identify the Loop: For any habit, break it down into its cue, routine, and reward.
2. Change the Routine: Replace a negative routine with a positive one that provides a similar reward.
3. Experiment with Rewards: Test different rewards to find what truly satisfies your craving.
4. Make It Obvious: Design your environment to highlight cues for good habits and hide cues for bad ones.

*Practical Exercise: Map Your Habit Loops*

Choose one habit you'd like to change or create. Use the following steps to map out its habit loop:
1. Cue: What triggers the habit?
2. Routine: What action do you take?
3. Reward: What benefit do you gain?

Once you've mapped the loop, brainstorm ways to tweak it. For example:

- If you want to stop snacking at night, identify the cue (e.g., watching TV) and replace the routine (e.g., drink tea instead).
- If you want to start exercising, create a cue (e.g., lay out your workout clothes the night before) and choose a reward (e.g., a smoothie after your workout).

**The Power of Awareness**

The first step to changing any habit is awareness. By understanding the habit loop, you can take control of your behaviors instead of letting them control you.

- Journaling: Keep a habit journal to track your cues, routines, and rewards.
- Reflection: At the end of each day, reflect on your habits and identify patterns.

**A Call to Action**

Now that you understand the habit loop, it's time to put it into practice. Choose one habit you'd like to change or create, and map out its loop. Then, experiment with tweaking the routine or reward to make the habit work for you.

Remember, habits are not destiny—they are patterns that can be reshaped. By mastering the habit loop, you can take control of your behaviors and create a life of purpose and growth.

**Final Thought**

The habit loop is a powerful tool for understanding and changing your behaviors. By identifying the cues, routines, and rewards that drive your habits, you can create positive change—one small shift at a time.

# Chapter 3: The Myth of Willpower

**The Story of the Marshmallow Test**
In the 1960s, psychologist Walter Mischel conducted a famous experiment known as the Marshmallow Test. Children were offered a choice: eat one marshmallow now or wait 15 minutes and receive two marshmallows. The study found that children who could delay gratification tended to have better life outcomes, such as higher SAT scores and lower rates of obesity.

This experiment is often cited as evidence of the power of willpower. But here's the catch: willpower is not a reliable strategy for long-term success. While some children resisted the marshmallow through sheer self-control, others used clever strategies, like covering their eyes or distracting themselves. In other words, they didn't rely on willpower—they relied on systems.

**What Is Willpower, and Why Does It Fail?**
Willpower is the ability to resist short-term temptations in pursuit of long-term goals. It's like a muscle: it can be strengthened with practice, but it also fatigues with overuse.

- The Problem with Willpower:
- Limited Resource: Willpower is finite. The more you use it, the more it depletes.
- Context-Dependent: Willpower is influenced by factors like stress, sleep, and hunger.

- Unreliable: Relying on willpower alone is like trying to hold your breath forever—it's unsustainable.

Research shows that people who rely on willpower to achieve their goals are more likely to fail. Instead of fighting temptation, the key is to design your environment and habits so that willpower becomes unnecessary.

**The Role of Environment in Habit Formation**

Your environment is one of the most powerful influences on your behavior. It shapes your cues, routines, and rewards—often without you even realizing it.

Cues in Your Environment:
- If you keep junk food on your kitchen counter, you're more likely to snack.
- If your phone is within reach, you're more likely to check it.

Designing a Supportive Environment:
- Make Good Habits Obvious: Place cues for positive habits in visible locations (e.g., lay out your workout clothes the night before).
- Make Bad Habits Invisible: Remove cues for negative habits (e.g., uninstall social media apps or hide unhealthy snacks).

Practical Exercise: Walk through your home or workspace and identify environmental cues that trigger your habits. How can you redesign your space to support your goals?

## The Power of Defaults

Defaults are the options that are automatically selected if you don't take action. They are incredibly powerful because most people stick with the default, even if it's not the best choice.

Examples of Defaults:
- Opting in vs. opting out of retirement savings plans.
- Pre-selected meal options on a flight.

How to Use Defaults to Your Advantage:
- Set up automatic transfers to your savings account.
- Pre-schedule workouts or meal prep sessions.

By making good habits the default, you reduce the need for willpower and decision-making.

## The Role of Friction in Habit Formation

Friction refers to the resistance or difficulty associated with a behavior. By reducing friction for good habits and increasing friction for bad ones, you can make positive behaviors effortless and negative behaviors difficult.

-Reducing Friction for Good Habits:
- Keep your gym bag packed and by the door.
- Use a habit-tracking app to simplify progress monitoring.

Increasing Friction for Bad Habits:
- Unplug your TV and store the remote in a drawer.
- Set a password on your phone to limit mindless scrolling.

Practical Exercise: Identify one good habit you want to adopt and one bad habit you want to break. How can you reduce friction for the good habit and increase friction for the bad one?

**The Role of Social Environment**

Your social environment—the people around you—also plays a critical role in shaping your habits.

The Power of Social Norms:
- If your friends exercise regularly, you're more likely to do the same.
- If your coworkers snack on junk food, you're more likely to join in.

How to Leverage Your Social Environment:
- Surround yourself with people who share your goals and values.
- Join communities or groups that support your desired habits.

Practical Exercise: Reflect on your social circle. Are there people who encourage or discourage your goals? How can you spend more time with those who support your growth?

## A Call to Action

Willpower is not the solution—it's the problem. Instead of relying on self-control, focus on designing your environment to make good habits inevitable and bad habits impossible.

- Start Small: Make one tiny change to your environment today.
- Experiment: Test different strategies to see what works for you.
- Iterate: Continuously refine your environment to support your goals.

## Final Thought

The myth of willpower is that it's the key to success. The truth is, success comes from designing systems that make good habits easy and bad habits hard. By taking control of your environment, you can create a life of purpose and growth—without relying on willpower.

# Chapter 4: Law 1 – Make It Obvious

### The Story of the Invisible Cues
Imagine walking into your kitchen and seeing a bowl of fresh fruit on the counter. Now imagine walking in and seeing a bag of chips instead. Which are you more likely to eat?

This simple example illustrates a powerful truth: your environment shapes your behavior. The cues around you—whether visible or invisible—trigger your habits, often without you even realizing it. To create new habits, you must first make the cues for those habits obvious.

### The Importance of Cues in Habit Formation
Cues are the triggers that initiate a habit. They can be external (like a time of day or a location) or internal (like an emotion or thought). Without a clear cue, a habit won't stick.

Why Cues Matter:
- They signal your brain to start a behavior.
- They create a link between your environment and your habits.
- They make habits automatic over time.

The first law of behavior change is to make it obvious. By designing your environment to highlight the cues for good habits, you can make those habits easier to adopt.

**How to Make Cues Obvious**

Here are four strategies for making the cues for your habits more visible:

*1. Use Implementation Intentions*

An implementation intention is a plan that specifies when, where, and how you will perform a habit. It's a simple but powerful tool for making cues obvious.

The Formula: "I will [BEHAVIOR] at [TIME] in [LOCATION]."
- Example: "I will meditate for 10 minutes at 7 a.m. in my living room."

Why It Works: Implementation intentions create a clear link between a specific cue (time and location) and a desired behavior.

Practical Exercise: Write down three implementation intentions for habits you want to build. Be as specific as possible.

*2. Design Your Environment*

Your environment is one of the most powerful influences on your behavior. By designing it to highlight the cues for good habits, you can make those habits easier to adopt.

Make Good Habits Visible:
- Place your running shoes by the door.
- Keep a water bottle on your desk.

- Put healthy snacks at eye level in the fridge.

Make Bad Habits Invisible:
- Hide junk food in the pantry.
- Unplug your TV and store the remote in a drawer.
- Delete social media apps from your phone.

Practical Exercise: Walk through your home or workspace and identify ways to make the cues for good habits more obvious and the cues for bad habits less visible.

*3. Use Habit Stacking*

Habit stacking is a technique that involves linking a new habit to an existing one. By "stacking" habits, you can use the cue from an existing habit to trigger a new one.

The Formula: "After [CURRENT HABIT], I will [NEW HABIT]."
- Example: "After I brush my teeth, I will floss."

Why It Works: Habit stacking leverages the power of existing cues to make new habits easier to adopt.

Practical Exercise: Identify three existing habits and stack a new habit onto each one.

*4. Create Visual Reminders*

Visual reminders are cues that prompt you to take action. They can be as simple as a sticky note or as elaborate as a vision board.

Examples of Visual Reminders:
- A sticky note on your mirror reminding you to practice gratitude.
- A calendar with workout days marked in red.
- A vision board with images of your goals.

Why It Works: Visual reminders keep your goals and habits top of mind, making it easier to take action.

Practical Exercise: Create a visual reminder for one habit you want to build. Place it somewhere you'll see it every day.

**The Role of Attention in Habit Formation**

Attention is the bridge between cues and habits. By paying attention to the cues around you, you can take control of your behaviors and create positive change.

- Mindfulness: Practice mindfulness to become more aware of your habits and the cues that trigger them.
- Reflection: At the end of each day, reflect on your habits and identify the cues that prompted them.

Practical Exercise: Spend one day tracking your habits and the cues that trigger them. Write down each habit and its corresponding cue.

**A Call to Action**

The first step to building new habits is to make the cues for those habits obvious. Start by designing your environment, using implementation intentions, and stacking habits. Remember, small changes can lead to big results over time.

- Start Small: Make one tiny change to your environment today.
- Experiment: Test different strategies to see what works for you.
- Iterate: Continuously refine your cues to support your goals.

**Final Thought**

Habits are not just about actions—they're about cues. By making the cues for good habits obvious, you can create a life of purpose and growth. So, what cue will you make obvious today?

# Chapter 5: Law 2 – Make It Attractive

### The Story of the Temptation Bundling

Imagine you love listening to podcasts but struggle to find time to exercise. What if you could combine the two? This is the idea behind temptation bundling—a strategy that links a habit you want to build with something you already enjoy.

For example, you could only allow yourself to listen to your favorite podcast while running. Over time, your brain begins to associate exercise with the pleasure of listening to the podcast, making the habit more attractive.

This story illustrates the second law of behavior change: Make It Attractive. The more appealing a habit is, the more likely you are to stick with it.

### The Role of Dopamine in Habit Formation

Dopamine is a neurotransmitter that plays a key role in motivation and reward. When you experience something pleasurable, your brain releases dopamine, which reinforces the behavior and makes you want to repeat it.

The Dopamine-Driven Feedback Loop:
1. Cue: You encounter a trigger (e.g., the smell of coffee).
2. Craving: Your brain anticipates a reward and releases dopamine.
3. Routine: You perform the behavior (e.g., drinking coffee).

4. Reward: You experience pleasure, reinforcing the habit.

By making habits more attractive, you can tap into this dopamine-driven feedback loop and create behaviors that stick.

**How to Make Habits Attractive**

Here are four strategies for making your habits more appealing:

*1. Use Temptation Bundling*

Temptation bundling is a technique that pairs a habit you want to build with something you already enjoy.

The Formula: "Only [HABIT YOU NEED] while [HABIT YOU WANT]."
- Example: "Only watch Netflix while on the treadmill."

Why It Works: Temptation bundling leverages the power of immediate rewards to make habits more attractive.

Practical Exercise: Identify one habit you want to build and one activity you enjoy. How can you bundle them together?

*2. Reframe Your Mindset*

The way you think about a habit can make it more or less attractive. By reframing your mindset, you can turn a chore into a choice.

Examples of Reframing:

- Instead of "I have to exercise," think "I get to improve my health."
- Instead of "I have to save money," think "I get to invest in my future."

- Why It Works: Reframing shifts your focus from the effort required to the benefits gained, making the habit more appealing.

Practical Exercise: Write down one habit you find unappealing and reframe it in a positive light.

### 3. Leverage Social Influence

Humans are social creatures, and we're heavily influenced by the people around us. By surrounding yourself with people who have the habits you want to adopt, you can make those habits more attractive.

The Power of Social Norms:
- If your friends exercise regularly, you're more likely to do the same.
- If your coworkers eat healthy, you're more likely to follow suit.

How to Leverage Social Influence:
- Join a community or group that shares your goals.
- Find an accountability partner to keep you motivated.

Practical Exercise: Identify one person or group that can support your habit goals. How can you spend more time with them?

*4. Create a Reward System*

Rewards make habits more attractive by providing immediate satisfaction. By creating a reward system, you can reinforce positive behaviors and make them more enjoyable.

Examples of Rewards:
- Treat yourself to a favorite snack after completing a workout.
- Allow yourself to watch an episode of your favorite show after finishing a task.

Why It Works: Rewards activate the brain's dopamine system, reinforcing the habit and making it more likely to stick.

Practical Exercise: Choose one habit you want to build and design a reward system to support it.

**The Role of Identity in Attractiveness**

The more a habit aligns with your identity, the more attractive it becomes. When you see yourself as the type of person who values health, productivity, or growth, your habits naturally become more appealing.

Examples of Identity-Based Habits:
- "I'm a runner" makes exercise more attractive.
- "I'm a reader" makes reading more appealing.

How to Leverage Identity:

- Focus on who you want to become, not just what you want to achieve.
- Use affirmations to reinforce your desired identity.

Practical Exercise: Write down one habit you want to build and how it aligns with your desired identity.

**A Call to Action**

The second law of behavior change is to Make It Attractive. By making your habits more appealing, you can tap into the power of dopamine and create behaviors that stick.

- Start Small: Make one tiny change to increase the attractiveness of a habit today.
- Experiment: Test different strategies to see what works for you.
- Iterate: Continuously refine your approach to make habits more enjoyable.

**Final Thought**

Habits are not just about actions—they're about desires. By making your habits more attractive, you can create a life of purpose and growth. So, what habit will you make more appealing today?

# Chapter 6: Law 3 – Make It Easy

### The Story of the Two-Minute Rule

Imagine you want to start a daily meditation practice, but the thought of sitting still for 30 minutes feels overwhelming. What if you started with just two minutes?

This is the idea behind the Two-Minute Rule: when starting a new habit, scale it down to a version that takes less than two minutes to complete. For example:
- "Read more" becomes "Read one page."
- "Run a marathon" becomes "Put on your running shoes."

The Two-Minute Rule works because it makes the habit easy to start. And once you've started, it's much easier to keep going.

This story illustrates the third law of behavior change: Make It Easy. The simpler a habit is, the more likely you are to stick with it.

### The Role of Friction in Habit Formation

Friction refers to the resistance or difficulty associated with a behavior. The more friction there is, the harder it is to perform a habit. Conversely, the less friction there is, the easier it is to perform a habit.

-Examples of Friction:
- A cluttered kitchen makes cooking harder.
- A complicated sign-up process makes joining a gym less likely.

How to Reduce Friction:
- Simplify the habit to its smallest possible version.
- Design your environment to make the habit effortless.

By reducing friction, you can make good habits easy and bad habits hard.

**How to Make Habits Easy**

Here are four strategies for making your habits easier to adopt:

*1. Start Small with the Two-Minute Rule*

The Two-Minute Rule is a powerful tool for overcoming procrastination and building momentum.

- The Formula: Scale down your habit to a version that takes less than two minutes to complete.
- Example: "Write a book" becomes "Write one sentence."
- Why It Works: Starting small removes the mental barrier to entry and makes it easier to build momentum.

Practical Exercise: Choose one habit you want to build and apply the Two-Minute Rule. What's the smallest version of the habit you can start with?

*2. Design Your Environment for Success*

Your environment plays a critical role in shaping your behavior. By designing it to reduce friction, you can make good habits effortless.

Make Good Habits Easy:
- Keep your workout clothes and shoes by the door.
- Pre-pack your lunch the night before.
- Use a habit-tracking app to simplify progress monitoring.

Make Bad Habits Hard:
- Unplug your TV and store the remote in a drawer.
- Delete social media apps from your phone.
- Keep junk food out of the house.

Practical Exercise: Walk through your home or workspace and identify ways to reduce friction for good habits and increase friction for bad ones.

*3. Use Habit Stacking*

Habit stacking is a technique that involves linking a new habit to an existing one. By "stacking" habits, you can leverage the momentum of an existing routine to make a new habit easier to adopt.

- The Formula: "After [CURRENT HABIT], I will [NEW HABIT]."
- Example: "After I brush my teeth, I will floss."

Why It Works: Habit stacking reduces the need for decision-making by tying the new habit to an existing cue.

Practical Exercise: Identify three existing habits and stack a new habit onto each one.

*4. Automate Your Habits*

Automation is the ultimate way to reduce friction. By setting up systems that perform habits for you, you can make them effortless.

Examples of Automation:
- Set up automatic transfers to your savings account.
- Use a meal delivery service to eat healthier.
- Schedule recurring reminders for your habits.

Why It Works: Automation removes the need for willpower and decision-making, making habits easier to maintain.

Practical Exercise: Choose one habit you want to automate and set up a system to support it.

**The Role of Consistency in Habit Formation**

Consistency is more important than intensity when it comes to building habits. By focusing on small, easy actions, you can create a foundation for lasting change.

-The Power of Repetition:
- The more you repeat a habit, the more automatic it becomes.

- Consistency builds momentum and makes it easier to scale up over time.

How to Stay Consistent:
- Start small and focus on showing up every day.
- Use a habit tracker to monitor your progress.

Practical Exercise: Choose one habit and commit to performing it consistently for 30 days. Start small and focus on building momentum.

**A Call to Action**

The third law of behavior change is to Make It Easy. By reducing friction and starting small, you can create habits that stick.

- Start Small: Apply the Two-Minute Rule to one habit today.
- Experiment: Test different strategies to see what works for you.
- Iterate: Continuously refine your approach to make habits easier.

**Final Thought**

Habits are not just about actions—they're about ease. By making your habits easy to start and maintain, you can create a life of purpose and growth. So, what habit will you make easier today?

# Chapter 7: Law 4 – Make It Satisfying

### The Story of the Gold Star System

Imagine a child learning to read. Every time they finish a book, they receive a gold star on a chart. Over time, the chart fills up with stars, and the child feels a sense of pride and accomplishment.

This simple reward system illustrates the fourth law of behavior change: Make It Satisfying. The more satisfying a habit is, the more likely you are to repeat it.

### The Role of Immediate Rewards in Habit Formation

Humans are wired to prioritize immediate rewards over delayed ones. This is why we often choose short-term pleasures (like eating junk food) over long-term benefits (like eating healthy).

The Problem with Delayed Rewards:
- The benefits of good habits (e.g., exercising, saving money) are often delayed.
- The costs of bad habits (e.g., smoking, overspending) are often immediate.

The Solution: To make good habits stick, you need to create immediate rewards that reinforce the behavior.

## How to Make Habits Satisfying

Here are four strategies for making your habits more satisfying:

*1. Use Immediate Rewards*

Immediate rewards provide instant gratification, making habits more enjoyable and reinforcing.

Examples of Immediate Rewards:
- Treat yourself to a favorite snack after completing a workout.
- Allow yourself to watch an episode of your favorite show after finishing a task.

Why It Works: Immediate rewards activate the brain's dopamine system, reinforcing the habit and making it more likely to stick.

Practical Exercise: Choose one habit you want to build and design an immediate reward to support it.

*2. Track Your Progress*

Tracking your progress provides a visual representation of your success, making habits more satisfying.

Examples of Progress Tracking:
- Use a habit tracker to mark each day you complete a habit.
- Keep a journal to record your achievements.

Why It Works: Progress tracking creates a sense of accomplishment and motivates you to keep going.

Practical Exercise: Choose one habit and start tracking your progress using a habit tracker or journal.

### 3. Celebrate Small Wins

Celebrating small wins reinforces positive behavior and makes habits more satisfying.

Examples of Celebrating Small Wins:
- Give yourself a high-five after completing a task.
- Share your achievements with a friend or family member.

Why It Works: Celebrating small wins creates positive emotions and reinforces the habit.

Practical Exercise: Choose one habit and commit to celebrating small wins along the way.

### 4. Use a Reward System

A reward system provides structured incentives for completing habits, making them more satisfying.

Examples of Reward Systems:
- Earn points for each habit completed and redeem them for a reward.

- Set up a savings jar and add money for each habit completed.

Why It Works: Reward systems create a clear link between behavior and reward, reinforcing the habit.

Practical Exercise: Choose one habit and design a reward system to support it.

**The Role of Identity in Satisfaction**
The more a habit aligns with your identity, the more satisfying it becomes. When you see yourself as the type of person who values health, productivity, or growth, your habits naturally become more rewarding.

Examples of Identity-Based Habits:
- "I'm a runner" makes exercise more satisfying.
- "I'm a reader" makes reading more rewarding.

How to Leverage Identity:
- Focus on who you want to become, not just what you want to achieve.
- Use affirmations to reinforce your desired identity.

Practical Exercise: Write down one habit you want to build and how it aligns with your desired identity.

## A Call to Action

The fourth law of behavior change is to Make It Satisfying. By creating immediate rewards and celebrating small wins, you can reinforce positive behavior and make habits stick.

- Start Small: Make one tiny change to increase the satisfaction of a habit today.
- Experiment: Test different strategies to see what works for you.
- Iterate: Continuously refine your approach to make habits more rewarding.

## Final Thought

Habits are not just about actions—they're about satisfaction. By making your habits more satisfying, you can create a life of purpose and growth. So, what habit will you make more rewarding today?

# Chapter 8: Breaking Bad Habits

### The Story of the Habit Loop Reversal
Imagine you have a habit of snacking late at night. Every evening, you find yourself reaching for a bag of chips, even though you know it's not good for you.

This story illustrates a common challenge: breaking bad habits. The key to overcoming them lies in understanding the habit loop—cue, routine, reward—and reversing it.

### The Science of Breaking Bad Habits
Breaking bad habits is not about willpower; it's about understanding and manipulating the habit loop.

The Habit Loop:
- Cue: The trigger that initiates the habit.
- Routine: The behavior or action you perform.
- Reward: The benefit or satisfaction you gain from the behavior.

The Problem with Bad Habits:
- They are often reinforced by immediate rewards (e.g., the pleasure of eating junk food).
- They are triggered by cues that are hard to avoid (e.g., stress, boredom).

The Solution: To break a bad habit, you need to identify the cue and reward, and then replace the routine with a healthier alternative.

**How to Break Bad Habits**

Here are four strategies for breaking bad habits:

*1. Identify the Cue and Reward*

The first step to breaking a bad habit is to understand what triggers it and what reward it provides.

How to Identify the Cue:
- Ask yourself: When, where, and why does the habit occur?
- Keep a habit journal to track the cues and rewards.

How to Identify the Reward:
- Ask yourself: What craving does the habit satisfy?
- Experiment with different rewards to find the true motivation.

Practical Exercise: Choose one bad habit and identify its cue and reward.

*2. Replace the Routine*

Once you understand the cue and reward, you can replace the routine with a healthier alternative that provides the same reward.

Examples of Routine Replacement:
- If you snack when stressed, try deep breathing or going for a walk instead.

- If you check your phone when bored, try reading a book or listening to music.

Why It Works: Replacing the routine maintains the same cue and reward, making it easier to break the habit.

Practical Exercise: Choose one bad habit and brainstorm healthier alternatives to replace the routine.

*3. Make the Bad Habit Harder to Perform*

Increasing friction for bad habits makes them harder to perform, reducing the likelihood of relapse.

Examples of Increasing Friction:
- Unplug your TV and store the remote in a drawer.
- Delete social media apps from your phone.
- Keep junk food out of the house.

Why It Works: Increasing friction reduces the temptation to perform the bad habit.

Practical Exercise: Choose one bad habit and identify ways to increase friction.

*4. Use a Reward System*

A reward system provides structured incentives for avoiding bad habits, making it easier to break them.

Examples of Reward Systems:
- Earn points for each day you avoid the bad habit and redeem them for a reward.
- Set up a savings jar and add money for each day you avoid the bad habit.

- Why It Works: Reward systems create a clear link between behavior and reward, reinforcing positive behavior.

Practical Exercise: Choose one bad habit and design a reward system to support breaking it.

**The Role of Environment in Breaking Bad Habits**

Your environment plays a critical role in shaping your behavior. By designing it to reduce cues for bad habits, you can make them easier to break.

Examples of Environmental Design:
- Remove cues for bad habits from your home or workspace.
- Surround yourself with people who support your goals.

Why It Works: Environmental design reduces the temptation to perform bad habits.

Practical Exercise: Walk through your home or workspace and identify ways to reduce cues for bad habits.

## A Call to Action

Breaking bad habits is not about willpower; it's about understanding and manipulating the habit loop. By identifying the cue and reward, replacing the routine, and increasing friction, you can create a life free from bad habits.

- Start Small: Choose one bad habit to break today.
- Experiment: Test different strategies to see what works for you.
- Iterate: Continuously refine your approach to make breaking bad habits easier.

## Final Thought

Bad habits are not destiny—they are patterns that can be reshaped. By understanding the habit loop and taking control of your environment, you can break free from bad habits and create a life of purpose and growth. So, what bad habit will you break today?

# Chapter 9: Dealing with Setbacks

### The Story of the Comeback

Imagine an athlete who suffers a major injury just before a big competition. Despite the setback, they work tirelessly to recover, eventually returning stronger than ever and winning the championship.

This story illustrates a powerful truth: setbacks are not the end—they are an opportunity for a comeback. The key to overcoming setbacks lies in resilience, adaptability, and a growth mindset.

### The Reality of Setbacks

Setbacks are an inevitable part of any journey. Whether it's missing a workout, breaking a diet, or falling back into a bad habit, everyone experiences setbacks.

Why Setbacks Happen:
- Life is unpredictable, and external factors (e.g., stress, illness) can disrupt your routine.
- Habits are not linear; progress often involves trial and error.

The Problem with Setbacks:
- They can lead to feelings of guilt, frustration, and self-doubt.
- They can derail progress if not handled properly.

The Solution: To overcome setbacks, you need to develop resilience and a plan for getting back on track.

## How to Deal with Setbacks

Here are four strategies for dealing with setbacks:

*1. Reframe Your Mindset*

The way you think about setbacks can make all the difference. By reframing your mindset, you can turn setbacks into opportunities for growth.

Examples of Reframing:
- Instead of "I failed," think "I learned something new."
- Instead of "This is too hard," think "This is a challenge I can overcome."

Why It Works: Reframing shifts your focus from failure to growth, making it easier to bounce back.

Practical Exercise: Write down one recent setback and reframe it in a positive light.

*2. Practice Self-Compassion*

Self-compassion involves treating yourself with kindness and understanding, especially during difficult times.

How to Practice Self-Compassion:
- Acknowledge your feelings without judgment.
- Remind yourself that setbacks are a normal part of the process.

- Treat yourself as you would treat a friend in the same situation.

Why It Works: Self-compassion reduces feelings of guilt and shame, making it easier to move forward.

Practical Exercise: Write a self-compassionate letter to yourself about a recent setback.

*3. Analyze the Setback*
Understanding the cause of a setback can help you prevent it from happening again.

How to Analyze a Setback:
- Identify the trigger (e.g., stress, lack of sleep).
- Reflect on what went wrong and what you can do differently next time.

Why It Works: Analysis provides insights that can help you improve and avoid future setbacks.

Practical Exercise: Choose one recent setback and analyze its cause. What can you do differently next time?

*4. Create a Comeback Plan*
A comeback plan provides a clear path for getting back on track after a setback.

How to Create a Comeback Plan:
- Set a specific goal for getting back on track.
- Break the goal down into small, manageable steps.
- Identify potential obstacles and how you'll overcome them.

Why It Works: A comeback plan provides structure and direction, making it easier to regain momentum.

Practical Exercise: Choose one habit you've struggled with and create a comeback plan.

### The Role of Support in Overcoming Setbacks

Support from others can make it easier to overcome setbacks. By surrounding yourself with people who encourage and motivate you, you can stay on track even when things get tough.

Examples of Support:
- Join a community or group that shares your goals.
- Find an accountability partner to keep you motivated.

Why It Works: Support provides encouragement and accountability, making it easier to bounce back.

Practical Exercise: Identify one person or group that can support you in overcoming setbacks.

**A Call to Action**

Setbacks are not the end—they are an opportunity for a comeback. By reframing your mindset, practicing self-compassion, analyzing the setback, and creating a comeback plan, you can overcome any obstacle.

- Start Small: Choose one setback to address today.
- Experiment: Test different strategies to see what works for you.
- Iterate: Continuously refine your approach to make overcoming setbacks easier.

**Final Thought**

Setbacks are a natural part of the journey, but they don't have to define you. By developing resilience and a growth mindset, you can turn setbacks into stepping stones for success. So, what setback will you overcome today?

# Chapter 10: From Tiny Shifts to Big Results

### The Story of the Compound Effect

Imagine planting a single seed in your garden. At first, it seems insignificant—just a tiny sprout breaking through the soil. But with consistent care, that seed grows into a towering tree, providing shade, beauty, and fruit for years to come.

This story illustrates the compound effect: the idea that small, consistent actions, over time, lead to extraordinary results. Just as a single seed can grow into a mighty tree, tiny shifts in your habits can transform your life.

### The Power of Consistency

Consistency is the key to unlocking the compound effect. While individual actions may seem small, their cumulative impact is profound.

Why Consistency Matters:
- Small actions, repeated consistently, create momentum.
- Over time, consistency builds habits that become automatic.

The Problem with Inconsistency:
- Inconsistent effort leads to sporadic results.
- Without consistency, even the best habits fail to stick.

The Solution: To achieve big results, focus on small, consistent actions.

**How to Achieve Big Results**

Here are four strategies for turning tiny shifts into big results:

*1. Focus on Systems, Not Goals*

Goals are important, but they are not enough. To achieve lasting success, you need to focus on systems—the processes and habits that lead to your goals.

Examples of Systems:
- Instead of setting a goal to lose 20 pounds, create a system of healthy eating and regular exercise.
- Instead of setting a goal to write a book, create a system of daily writing.

Why It Works: Systems provide a clear path for consistent action, making it easier to achieve your goals.

Practical Exercise: Choose one goal and create a system to support it.

*2. Embrace the Plateau of Latent Potential*

Progress is not always linear. Often, you'll experience a plateau of latent potential—a period where it feels like nothing is happening, even though you're putting in the effort.

Why Plateaus Happen:
- Results take time to manifest.

- Early efforts build the foundation for future success.

How to Overcome Plateaus:
- Trust the process and stay consistent.
- Focus on the habits, not just the outcomes.

Practical Exercise: Reflect on a time when you experienced a plateau. How did you overcome it?

*3. Track Your Progress*

Tracking your progress provides a visual representation of your success, making it easier to stay consistent.

Examples of Progress Tracking:
- Use a habit tracker to mark each day you complete a habit.
- Keep a journal to record your achievements.

Why It Works: Progress tracking creates a sense of accomplishment and motivates you to keep going.

Practical Exercise: Choose one habit and start tracking your progress using a habit tracker or journal.

*4. Celebrate Small Wins*

Celebrating small wins reinforces positive behavior and keeps you motivated.

Examples of Celebrating Small Wins:
- Give yourself a high-five after completing a task.
- Share your achievements with a friend or family member.

Why It Works: Celebrating small wins creates positive emotions and reinforces the habit.

Practical Exercise: Choose one habit and commit to celebrating small wins along the way.

**The Role of Patience in Achieving Big Results**

Patience is essential for achieving big results. While it's tempting to seek quick fixes, lasting success takes time.

Why Patience Matters:
- Real change is a slow, gradual process.
- Patience allows you to stay consistent, even when progress feels slow.

How to Cultivate Patience:
- Focus on the process, not just the outcomes.
- Remind yourself that small actions compound over time.

Practical Exercise: Write down one habit you're working on and remind yourself to be patient with the process.

**A Call to Action**

Big results come from tiny shifts. By focusing on systems, embracing plateaus, tracking your progress, and celebrating small wins, you can create a life of purpose and growth.

- Start Small: Choose one tiny shift to make today.
- Experiment: Test different strategies to see what works for you.
- Iterate: Continuously refine your approach to make achieving big results easier.

**Final Thought**

Tiny shifts may seem insignificant at first, but their power lies in their consistency. By focusing on small, manageable actions, you can create a life of extraordinary results. So, what tiny shift will you make today?

# Chapter 11: Building Systems, Not Goals

### The Story of the Marathon Runner

Imagine two people training for a marathon. Runner A sets a goal: "I want to finish the marathon in under four hours." They focus on the outcome, pushing themselves to train hard every day. But when progress feels slow, they get discouraged and eventually quit.

Runner B takes a different approach. Instead of focusing on the marathon, they focus on becoming a runner. They create a system of daily training, gradually increasing their mileage and improving their endurance. Over time, they not only complete the marathon but also adopt a new identity: "I am a runner."

This story illustrates a fundamental truth: goals are important, but systems are what lead to lasting success.

### The Problem with Goals

Goals are a destination, but they don't provide a roadmap for getting there. While they can be motivating, they also have several limitations:

- Goals are finite: Once you achieve a goal, the motivation often disappears.
- Goals can be overwhelming: Big goals can feel daunting, leading to procrastination or burnout.
- Goals don't address the process: They focus on the outcome, not the habits and systems needed to achieve it.

The Solution: To achieve lasting success, focus on building systems—the processes and habits that lead to your goals.

**How to Build Systems**

Here are four strategies for building systems that lead to lasting success:

*1. Focus on the Process, Not the Outcome*

The process is what leads to the outcome. By focusing on the process, you can create sustainable habits that lead to long-term success.

Examples of Process-Focused Systems:
- Instead of setting a goal to lose 20 pounds, create a system of healthy eating and regular exercise.
- Instead of setting a goal to write a book, create a system of daily writing.

Why It Works: Focusing on the process makes it easier to stay consistent and build momentum.

Practical Exercise: Choose one goal and create a system to support it.

*2. Design Your Environment for Success*

Your environment plays a critical role in shaping your behavior. By designing it to support your systems, you can make good habits effortless.

Make Good Habits Easy:

- Keep your workout clothes and shoes by the door.
- Pre-pack your lunch the night before.
- Use a habit-tracking app to simplify progress monitoring.

Make Bad Habits Hard:
- Unplug your TV and store the remote in a drawer.
- Delete social media apps from your phone.
- Keep junk food out of the house.

Practical Exercise: Walk through your home or workspace and identify ways to design your environment to support your systems.

## 3. Use Habit Stacking

Habit stacking is a technique that involves linking a new habit to an existing one. By "stacking" habits, you can leverage the momentum of an existing routine to make a new habit easier to adopt.

- The Formula: "After [CURRENT HABIT], I will [NEW HABIT]."
- Example: "After I brush my teeth, I will floss."

Why It Works: Habit stacking reduces the need for decision-making by tying the new habit to an existing cue.

Practical Exercise: Identify three existing habits and stack a new habit onto each one.

## 4. Automate Your Systems

Automation is the ultimate way to reduce friction and make your systems effortless. By setting up systems that perform habits for you, you can make them easier to maintain.

Examples of Automation:
- Set up automatic transfers to your savings account.
- Use a meal delivery service to eat healthier.
- Schedule recurring reminders for your habits.

Why It Works: Automation removes the need for willpower and decision-making, making habits easier to maintain.

Practical Exercise: Choose one habit you want to automate and set up a system to support it.

### The Role of Identity in Systems

The more a system aligns with your identity, the more sustainable it becomes. When you see yourself as the type of person who values health, productivity, or growth, your systems naturally align with those values.

Examples of Identity-Based Systems:
- "I'm a runner" makes exercise systems more sustainable.
- "I'm a writer" makes writing systems more appealing.

How to Leverage Identity:

- Focus on who you want to become, not just what you want to achieve.
- Use affirmations to reinforce your desired identity.

Practical Exercise: Write down one system you want to build and how it aligns with your desired identity.

**A Call to Action**

Goals are important, but systems are what lead to lasting success. By focusing on the process, designing your environment, using habit stacking, and automating your systems, you can create a life of purpose and growth.

- Start Small: Choose one system to build today.
- Experiment: Test different strategies to see what works for you.
- Iterate: Continuously refine your approach to make your systems more effective.

**Final Thought**

Systems are the bridge between where you are and where you want to be. By focusing on building systems, not just setting goals, you can create a life of lasting success. So, what system will you build today?

# Conclusion: The Ripple Effect of Tiny Shifts

### The Story of the Pebble in the Pond
Imagine tossing a pebble into a still pond. At first, the impact seems small—just a few ripples spreading outward. But as those ripples expand, they touch every corner of the pond, creating a wave of motion that transforms the entire surface.

This story illustrates the ripple effect: the idea that small, intentional actions can create far-reaching changes. Just as a single pebble can transform a pond, tiny shifts in your habits can transform your life.

### The Power of Tiny Shifts
Throughout this book, we've explored the science and strategies behind habit formation. From understanding the habit loop to building systems that support your goals, the key takeaway is clear: small, consistent actions lead to extraordinary results.

Why Tiny Shifts Work:
- They are manageable and sustainable.
- They compound over time, creating a ripple effect of positive change.

The Problem with Overwhelm:
- Big goals can feel daunting, leading to procrastination or burnout.
- Without small, consistent actions, progress stalls.

The Solution: Focus on tiny shifts—small, manageable changes that create momentum and lead to lasting success.

### The Ripple Effect in Action

The ripple effect of tiny shifts can be seen in every area of life:

- Health: A daily walk leads to improved fitness, energy, and mood.
- Productivity: A morning routine sets the tone for a focused, productive day.
- Relationships: Small acts of kindness strengthen bonds and build trust.
- Finances: Saving a little each day grows into a substantial nest egg over time.

By focusing on tiny shifts, you can create a ripple effect that transforms not just your habits but your entire life.

### The Role of Consistency

Consistency is the engine that drives the ripple effect. While individual actions may seem small, their cumulative impact is profound.

Why Consistency Matters:
- Small actions, repeated consistently, create momentum.
- Over time, consistency builds habits that become automatic.

How to Stay Consistent:
- Focus on systems, not just goals.

- Celebrate small wins to stay motivated.

Practical Exercise: Reflect on one tiny shift you've made and how it has created a ripple effect in your life.

**The Importance of Patience**

Patience is essential for seeing the ripple effect of tiny shifts. While it's tempting to seek quick fixes, lasting success takes time.

Why Patience Matters:
- Real change is a slow, gradual process.
- Patience allows you to stay consistent, even when progress feels slow.

How to Cultivate Patience:
- Focus on the process, not just the outcomes.
- Remind yourself that small actions compound over time.

Practical Exercise: Write down one habit you're working on and remind yourself to be patient with the process.

**A Call to Action**

The journey of a thousand miles begins with a single step. You don't need to have it all figured out to start making changes. In fact, the best way to make progress is to start small and build momentum.

- Start Small: Choose one tiny shift to make today.

- Experiment: Test different strategies to see what works for you.
- Iterate: Continuously refine your approach to make achieving big results easier.

**Final Thought**

Tiny shifts may seem insignificant at first, but their power lies in their consistency. By focusing on small, manageable actions, you can create a life of extraordinary results. So, what tiny shift will you make today?

www.ingramcontent.com/pod-product-compliance
Lightning Source LLC
Chambersburg PA
CBHW070439010526
44118CB00014B/2105